Dedication

This book is dedicated to the
prayer warriors whose prayers hold lives,
relationships, families, businesses, cultures,
nations and society together.

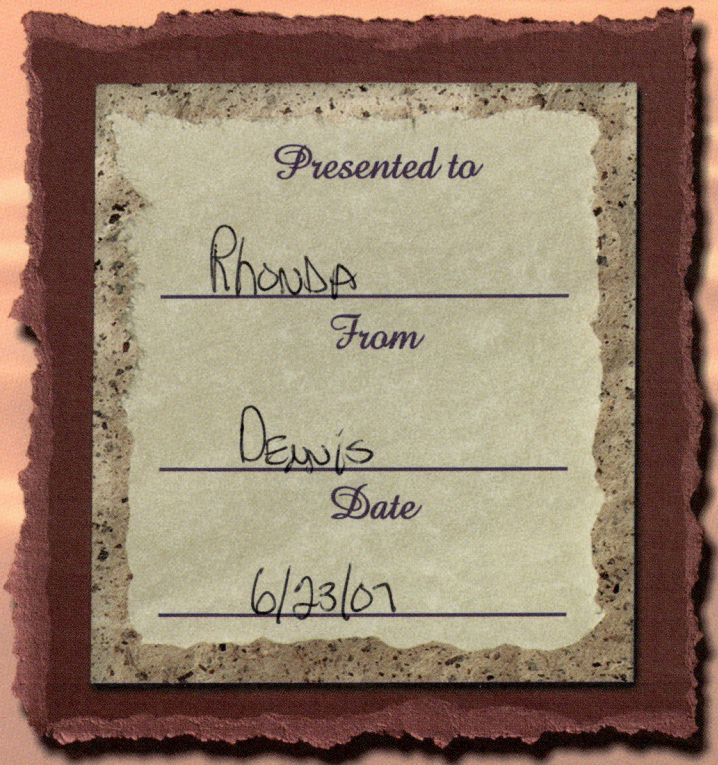

In every applicable instance, the author has personally paraphrased biblical characters, authors and texts in an attempt to make this book more readily understood in modern language. Quotations are not exact.

Written by Patty and Cecil O. Kemp, Jr.
Edited by Denise Hildreth
Art Direction by McClearen Design Studios, Nashville, Tennessee

The Wisdom Company, Inc.
P.O. Box 681351, Franklin, TN 37068-1351   1-800-728-1145

© 2000, by The Wisdom Company, Inc.
All rights reserved. No part of this book may be reproduced or transmitted in any form or by any means, electronic or mechanical, including photocopying, recording, or by any information storage and retrieval system, without written permission of The Wisdom Company, Inc.
ISBN# 1-893668-16-9
The Hope Collection is a brand and registered trade name of The Wisdom Company, Inc.

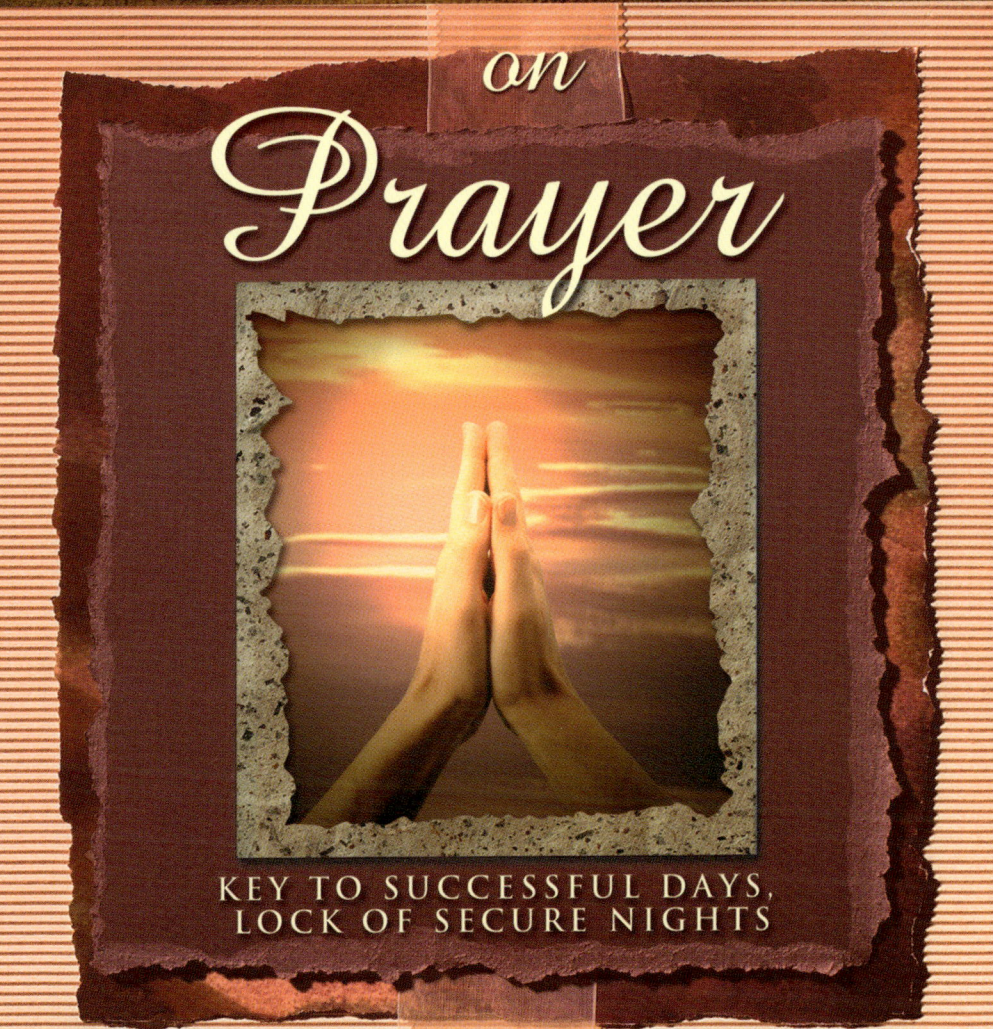

ABOUT THE HOPE COLLECTION

The Hope Collection books are based on the message of Real Hope shared in Cecil O. Kemp, Jr.'s acclaimed inspirational books; **Wisdom Honor & Hope** *(The Inner Path to True Greatness)* and **Wisdom & Money** *(The 7 Laws of Highest Prosperity)*.

THE HOPE COLLECTION INCLUDES:

Mothers *(Celebrate The Joy of Children)*

Students *(Dream Big! Dream Wisely!)*

Retirement *(The Best Years are Ahead)*

Storms *(Healing Words for Troubled Times)*

True Greatness *(26 Keys to Highest & Lasting Success)*

A Better Life *(Inspiration Today from Reflecting Back & Looking Within)*

Shaping a Life of Honor *(How To Live A Life of True Excellence)*

Lasting Peace *(Inspiring Thoughts for Possessing Real Hope & Security)*

Loving Unconditionally *(The Power & Passion for Living Life Fully)*

Higher Connection *(Truth, Inspiration & Wisdom for the Searching Soul)*

Relationship Heartaches *(Wisdom & Inspiration for Mending Broken Hearts)*

Forgiven *(The Healing Power of Forgiveness)*

Leaders *(86 Day Guidebook to Leadership Greatness)*

Prayer *(Key To Successful Days, Lock of Secure Nights)*

Abiding Faith *(Rediscovering the Rock of a Meaningful Life)*

Parents *(Inspiration & Wisdom For Successful Parenting)*

ABOUT THE CREATOR OF THE HOPE COLLECTION

Cecil O. Kemp, Jr. lived his dream, becoming a successful businessman and business owner. Yet, he was very unfulfilled. Enormous material success didn't deliver on its promises of hope and happiness. He set out to discover the secrets of a genuinely happy, hopeful life. Finding and applying them, he freed himself and his family from the rat race life, while enjoying even greater material success. After nearly two decades of this higher prosperity, he and his fellow writing friends offer those amazing discoveries in The Hope Collection.

Special Thanks

As you soak in the beauty, power and warmth of this and other Hope Collection books, remember these are the work of some very talented, special people. Special thanks to McClearen Design Studios, Anderson - Thomas Design, Wes Yoder and Ron Miller at Ambassador Agency, Kathryn Knight, B.J. Rogers, Stephen von Hagel and Robert Keifer.

Foreword

Modern society distracts us from life's most important activities, enticing us to fill our emptiness with

SWEET HOUR OF PRAYER! SWEET HOUR OF PRAYER! THAT CALLS ME FROM A WORLD OF CARE, AND BIDS ME AT MY FATHER'S THRONE. MAKE ALL MY WANTS AND WISHES KNOWN. IN SEASONS OF DISTRESS AND GRIEF, MY SOUL HAS OFTEN FOUND RELIEF.
—William A. Walford

things like work, entertainment, and recreation—each necessary, but none eternal.

Inner emptiness can only truly be filled when we allow God to live within us and continually commune with Him through three key spiritual activities—prayer, Scripture reading and meditation.

The power of prayer is a key to achieving true success.

The answers to life's questions and problems are found in personal communion with God. Through prayer, God gives us answers and imparts strength and hope for the day and the future—sustaining us and helping us do the important things of daily living and working.

> THINGS THAT MATTER MOST MUST NEVER BE AT THE MERCY OF THINGS WHICH MATTER LEAST.
> —*Johann Wolfgang von Goethe*

Only with prayer is it possible to walk with Divine guidance, inner peace and hope.

In the quest for life meaning, prayer is the catalyst for highest discovery. We encounter God at every turn, but prayer is surely the means of purest personal meeting. It is not simply a way to "ask" for things. Prayer is primarily a way to communicate and connect with God and to express our gratitude to Him for life and all its blessings so wonderfully and freely given us.

Prayer is a form of surrender to God's influence and wisdom. It is restorative–recharging the batteries and refocusing vision. Prayer calms the mind and broadens the recesses and reservoirs of our heart. It enables God's children to receive and retain the riches He has for us.

Prayer requires no physical tools, no academic brilliance, no perfect "words" and not even a perfect "heart." Prayer helps us strike a proper balance between Heaven's daily calling to introspection and Earth's practical life.

Prayer is a higher work of love. Each act of love is a prayer and an answer for someone. Prayer and loving deeds are excellent ways to translate our spiritual beliefs into practical action in the everyday world we live. And, faith and prayer are dynamic, spiritual twins that in daily practice allow us to overcome feelings of inadequacy, doubt, fear and loneliness.

Daily communing with God, we find rest from life's cares and demands. In prayer, our faith reaches up and God reaches down, giving us His power, peace, hope, tranquility and love needed for victorious living–regardless of momentary circumstance.

We cannot live life to its fullest nor create a legacy of honor without honestly caring about our own spiritual walk, the welfare of others, and always doing what is right. This can only be achieved by continually turning inward to distill, reflect, evaluate–and commune with God through prayer, Scripture reading and meditation.

It is important to spend our time wisely, because our life is currency we are privileged to spend only once. The most enjoyable, satisfying and refreshing place found in this life is with God in prayer. Thus, it is wise to spend much time in that place.

Jesus thought prayer was a priority over sleeping, eating or working. He conscientiously developed and maintained the habits of prayer, Scripture reading and meditation. It was his daily custom to rise a long time before daybreak, go to a solitary place and there alone with God, he prayed. It was not uncommon for him to pray all night long.

Silence, prayer, faith, love, service and peace were the six connected steps along the path of Mother Teresa's life. About their connectedness, she taught: Prayer is the fruit of silence, faith the fruit of prayer, love the fruit of faith, service the fruit of love and peace the fruit of service.

Do you think maybe Jesus and Mother Teresa were on to something very important, in stressing the power, priority and value of prayer–personal communion of the soul with God?

THE LIFE CHANGING POWER OF PRAYER IS REAL.

Consider two stories from a prayer warrior I know well, my wife Patty.

What's faster than a speeding bullet and can leap tall buildings in a single bound? SUPERMAN! Everyone loves him because he does the impossible and always shows up just in time to save the day! However, Superman does have one flaw—he's fictional.

However, there is someone faster than a speeding bullet who jumps tall buildings in a single bound. He is supernatural—but He is real and really does come on the scene when He is called upon! I know this from countless personal experiences, like these two.

When our daughter Heather was in the fourth grade she became very sick with Rocky Mountain Spotted Fever. Her temperature remained at a frightening 105 degrees for several days, regardless of what I attempted.

I awoke at three o'clock one morning feeling an urgency to pray for her. Her temperature was still 105, so I placed my hands upon her body and prayed for a miracle. Fifteen minutes later I took her temperature again. It had dropped to 102! I knew that God heard and answered my prayer. Medicine and science affirmed my faith when a blood test 15 years later proved Heather not only had RMSF, but antibodies still in her blood stream revealed she had survived a normally lethal case. God had truly been our "Superman" showing up just in time to save the day!

My Grandmother Robertson was a woman of prayer. She had a powerful influence on me and many others, though she never traveled more than a few miles from her rural Mississippi farm. She appeared a simple, ordinary person by society's standards, yet she made this world a better place to live.

Three times a day, she would slip away to a special place outside her house to be alone with God. Briefly escaping the clamor of raising eleven children, cooking meals, cleaning house, and dozens of other responsibilities–she would read The Bible, mediate, reflect and tell God of her own needs as well as others'. Those times were her priority. And because of that dedication, she influenced lives and saw God change them.

Sometimes I try to use my busy schedule to justify not spending time alone with God. When I do, I am reminded Grandmother Robertson didn't. Her example is frozen in my memory, reminding me to never get so busy I neglect "alone time"–and Reflection–with God–which brings everything into proper perspective.

Now, I understand the value of something Grandmother Robertson often said, paraphrasing St. Paul: With prayer and thanksgiving make your requests known to God and the peace of God will come on wings from heaven to keep your heart and mind, through anything and no matter what comes.

Thanks Patty, for those inspiring stories. Prayer changes things, bigtime! It brings us Real Hope and power needed to live every day optimistically confident and without fear or worry of what may or may not happen. In the midst of change, difficulties or success, by taking refuge in God, we can rest, find peace and refreshment and discover new strengths.

In prayer and meditation, we connect directly to God's thoughts and ways. Meditation on those nurtures the inner life of the spirit. A vibrant inner spirit is one connected directly to God. Through this connection flows peace beyond understanding that keeps the heart calm and quietly confident, even in troubled times. A sound mind grows from a heart at peace, inspired by Divine Wisdom.

Be still, rest your mind, listen to the beating of your heart, find the peace from above that is undisturbed by worry. Breathe in and live the peace, tranquility, strength and Hope of prayer and meditation on Eternal Truth.

DAILY LIVING

Prayer is the best preparation for daily living and working.

Being content with life means knowing God's purpose and plan for our lives, accepting these, and joyfully working to fulfill them.

Prayer is the filling station of divine contentment, knowledge, and joy.

Looking up daily, we can be led safely along the path to the far horizon and the realization of today's dreams and deepest hopes.

LET YOUR FIRST "GOOD MORNING" BE TO YOUR FATHER IN HEAVEN.
— *Karl G. Maeser*

IF YOU BEGIN TO LIVE LIFE LOOKING FOR THE GOD THAT IS ALL AROUND YOU, EVERY MOMENT BECOMES A PRAYER.
— *Frank Bianco*

IT IS FROM PRAYER THAT THE SPIRIT'S VICTORY SPRINGS.
— *Schillerbuch*

GET INTO THE HABIT OF DEALING WITH GOD ABOUT EVERYTHING. UNLESS IN THE FIRST WAKING MOMENT OF THE DAY YOU LEARN TO FLING THE DOOR WIDE BACK AND LET GOD IN, YOU WILL WORK ON A WRONG LEVEL ALL DAY; BUT SWING THE DOOR WIDE OPEN AND PRAY TO YOUR FATHER IN SECRET, AND EVERY PUBLIC THING WILL BE STAMPED WITH THE PRESENCE OF GOD.
— *Oswald Chambers*

Alone time with God brings everything into proper perspective.

Being alone regularly can be a wonderful gift. It's a great opportunity to learn more about ourselves, others and to listen to God.

Our life is a self-portrait of the philosophy and habits we choose for daily living and working. Devout prayer warriors develop the best portraits.

There's always a best way of doing everything. So it is with beginnings. Begin by looking up, reflecting, and then looking forward. Begin with the best in heart and mind. Begin with prayer and faith that looks up first, to be reminded of the good, value, and promise in all situations and people.

PRAYER IS NOT A LAST EXTREMITY, IT'S A FIRST NECESSITY.
—Unknown

IF YOU CAN'T SLEEP, DON'T COUNT SHEEP. TALK TO THE SHEPHERD.
—Unknown

SEVEN PRAYERLESS DAYS MAKE ONE WEAK.
—Unknown

LET EVERYONE TRY AND FIND THAT AS A RESULT OF DAILY PRAYER HE ADDS SOMETHING NEW TO HIS LIFE, SOMETHING WITH WHICH NOTHING CAN BE COMPARED.
—Mahatma Gandhi

PRAYER CATAPULTS US ONTO THE FRONTIER OF THE SPIRITUAL LIFE. OF ALL THE SPIRITUAL DISCIPLINES PRAYER IS THE MOST CENTRAL....REAL PRAYER IS LIFE CREATING AND LIFE CHANGING...
—Richard Foster

Wise habits like prayer are the means our spirit person uses to carry us to freedom and security.

A spiritually wise heart and devout prayer life are essential to healthy bodies, emotions, thoughts, attitudes, and relationships.

> WE FIRST MAKE OUR HABITS, AND THEN OUR HABITS MAKE US.
> —*John Dryden*

Listening for and to God are life's best habits.

Nothing compares to the promise of your life lived in partnership with God

We are capable of choosing more wisely. It takes prayer and practice, but each of us can cultivate the habit.

We are wise to learn to live daily, by the vision seen in moments of prayer, meditation introspection and inspiration.

Our lives can and should express God's loving kindness, mercy, justice, honor and humility, inspiration and hope. In daily prayer, Scripture reading and meditation, those Divine qualities cannot help but rub off on us.

> REDEEM YOUR PRECIOUS TIME: PICK UP THE FRAGMENTS OF IT, THAT NOT ONE MOMENT OF IT MAY BE LOST. BE MUCH IN SECRET PRAYER. CONVERSE LESS WITH MAN, AND MORE WITH GOD.
> —*George Whitefield*

> NO HEART CAN CONCEIVE THAT TREASURY OF MERCIES WHICH LIES IN THIS ONE PRIVILEGE, IN HAVING LIBERTY AND ABILITY TO APPROACH UNTO GOD AT ALL TIMES, ACCORDING TO HIS MIND AND WILL.
> —*John Owen*

The prayers of one who is living right and praying diligently are very effective.

Eternal Truth is the only compass we need for daily living.

Frequently we pray that God would not forsake us in the hour of trial and temptation, but we too much forget that we have need to use this prayer at all times. There is no moment of our life, however holy, in which we can do without His constant upholding. Whether in light or in darkness, in communion or in temptation, we alike need the prayer,

> "FORSAKE ME NOT, O LORD. HOLD THOU ME UP, AND I SHALL BE SAFE."
> —*C. H. Spurgeon*

FEAR

Denial blindfolds pain and blocks the path to progress. Recognize your fear—this is wise. Learn from and release your fear in faith and prayer—this is honorable. Believe that a better life awaits—this is hopeful.

You are never truly alone. God's Spirit is always with you.

PRAYER SHOULD BE THE KEY OF THE DAY AND THE LOCK OF THE NIGHT.
—*Thomas Fuller*

DON'T WORRY ABOUT ANYTHING; INSTEAD, PRAY ABOUT EVERYTHING; TELL THE DIVINE YOUR NEEDS AND DON'T FORGET TO THANK HIM FOR HIS ANSWERS. IF YOU DO THIS, YOU WILL EXPERIENCE GOD'S PEACE WHICH IS FAR MORE WONDERFUL THAN THE HUMAN MIND CAN UNDERSTAND. GOD'S PEACE WILL KEEP YOUR THOUGHTS AND YOUR HEARTS QUIET AND AT REST, AS YOU TRUST IN THE LORD. THE SECRET TO PEACE WITH CONTENTMENT IN EVERY SITUATION IS BELIEVING WE CAN DO ANYTHING, WITH THE GREAT HELP OF GOD WHO GIVES US THE REQUISITE STRENGTH AND POWER.
—*St. Paul*

PRAYER IS THE SONG OF THE HEART. IT REACHES THE EAR OF GOD EVEN IF IT IS MINGLED WITH THE CRY AND THE TUMULT OF A THOUSAND MEN.
—*Kahlil Gibran*

Pray in times of trouble and need, to receive help and assure faith is built.

Inner strength is one of the many products of a devout prayer life. This strength can fortify our emotions and see us through the most difficult of times.

SOMETIMES WE EXPECT MILLION $ ANSWERS FROM 10 CENT PRAYERS.
—Unknown

When suffering, pray about it. Keep on praying, until the answer comes.

Pray in times of prosperity, to avoid the temptations to becoming faithless and proud.

SNUGGLE IN GOD'S ARMS. WHEN YOU ARE HURTING, WHEN YOU FEEL LONELY, LEFT OUT...LET HIM CRADLE YOU, COMFORT YOU, REASSURE YOU OF HIS ALL-SUFFICIENT POWER AND LOVE.
—Kay Arthur

Pray in times of security, to avoid the temptation of becoming self-sufficient.

Pray in times of danger, to overcome doubts and fears.

> WHERE THERE IS PEACE AND MEDITATION, THERE IS NEITHER ANXIETY NOR DOUBT.
> —St. Francis of Assisi

> YOU PRAY IN YOUR DISTRESS AND IN YOUR NEED; WOULD THAT YOU MIGHT ALSO PMNJ;LOF ABUNDANCE.
> —Kahlil Gibran

Patience acknowledges that God is in control and that things are just as they need to be, right now, this moment, even if we are not able to see the purpose in all that is going on around us.

> GOD'S THOUGHTS AND WAYS ARE HIGHER THAN OURS, AS FAR AS HEAVEN IS ABOVE EARTH.
> —*The Old Testament Prophet Isaiah*

In prayer, Scripture reading and meditation, we connect directly to God's thoughts and ways.

> YOU CANNOT FIX PROBLEMS WITH THE SAME LEVEL OF THINKING THAT CREATED THEM.
> —*Albert Einstein*

Effective faith is faith that endures, even through doubts.

Life's blessings prove God's greatness and that He indeed answers prayer.

> OUR DILEMMA GOES DEEPER THAN SHORTAGE OF TIME; IT IS BASICALLY A PROBLEM OF PRIORITIES. WE HAVE LEFT UNDONE THESE THINGS WE OUGHT TO HAVE DONE.
> —*Charles Hummel*

As you pray, cut God some slack on the answer timetable. Remember that in His time, The Divine mends broken hearts, dreams, lives, relationships and families.

> MORE THINGS ARE WROUGHT BY PRAYER/THAN THIS WORLD DREAMS OF.
> —*Lord Alfred Tennyson*

The storms of life often disguise the strengths we will discover from them and the blessings their lessons will lead us to in the future. Though it may take time before you understand today's difficulties, you can grow from them as you pray and move into a brighter, better future.

Grieving is personal, an important part of the healing process. Denying grief gives it power.

Instead of living in denial of the pain of loss, honor your grief, feel your pain and acknowledge it to yourself, and, if you feel comfortable doing so, to trusted loved ones. Most importantly, pour your heart out to God. All those actions can help clear the way for new opportunities. Use your grief to heal the hurts of the past and prepare for the dreams of the future.

God calms life's storms, stills the waves and brings us safely to harbor.

In vital union with God, we can trust Him for solutions to each day's problems.

Releasing our cares to God, we are rewarded with peaceful sleep, in the comfort, security and safety of Divine care.

God is very close to the one whose heart is breaking, always within whispering distance.

> NEVER WAS A FAITHFUL PRAYER LOST. SOME PRAYERS HAVE A LONGER VOYAGE THAN OTHERS, BUT THEN THEY RETURN WITH THEIR RICHER LADING AT LAST, SO THAT THE PRAYING SOUL IS A GAINER BY WAITING FOR AN ANSWER.
> —*William Gurnall*

> PRAYER IS: .... THE SALVE ON THE WOUNDS OF OUR SPIRIT THAT WE ORDER FROM GOD IN OUR MOMENTS WITH HIM.
> —*Unknown*

When walking through dark valleys, God is close beside, guarding and guiding all the way.

God is our high tower of refuge, our place of safety in the day of distress.

Rest in the night, covered by Eternal wings.

Bridle the doubts and fears that block your vision and courage. Pray to God and put on the bridle of faith in Him that removes doubts and fears, restoring higher vision and hope.

We can choose not to let negative ideas, fears, and perceptions of the external world limit us.

We can choose the freedom to test those limits, spread our wings, and fly. Do something constructive. Pray to God and invite freedom–from doubt, anger and the pain of the past–to enter your life!

DON'T WORRY.

Easier said than done?

How can you be at peace, free of anxiety?

Consider again the stories shared by my wife Patty, back in the first topic of this book.

In those, you learned that she was very concerned about our daughter, Heather. Patty knew she could not alter the situation, in her own power. So, she tapped the one power that indeed can change circumstances. She prayed and trusted God. THEN, peace came, you might say on the wings of prayer.

Faith and worry are incompatible. Worry negates faith and vice versa. When we worry, we destroy the single-minded concentration it takes to follow Wisdom's instructions on faith, prayer and making choices based on the principles, values and priorities of Eternal Truth.

Wisdom's pages are clear that we are to give the cares of life to God, in faith through prayer. By give, I mean in prayer, release your worries to God and go your way in faith, knowing your concerns are in the most skilled hands in the universe.

Another promise on the pages of Wisdom is that God always works out everything for good to those who are in harmonious, personal relationship and partnership with God. It may not turn out the way we thought it should, but God promises it will be good for all concerned. So, as you pray and daily release worries to God, stand steadfast in faith on that promise.

I would be remiss if I didn't mention two additional thoughts on worry.

First, we often worry over things that never could reasonably occur. Other times, we worry because we know the choices we have made and the actions we have taken were unwise. When Wisdom is not inside, fear causes great inner distress. Many respond to the distress by manipulating others and by behaviors that create problems or compound problems caused by unwise choices. Worry can not change a choice already made. Accompanied by unwise behavior, worry only assures things go from bad to worse.

In summary, instead of worrying or remaining anxious about anything, my suggestions are:

1. Read the Bible every day. Meditate on what you read.

2. Pray. Begin each prayer with thanksgiving. Then, release cares and concerns to God.

3. Have faith in God. Believe that God works things out for good in His time.

4. Receive the peace of God.

5. Take St. Paul's advice. Think on good, noble and pure things.

6. Consider the inspiring thoughts shared in this book.

7. Make spiritually wise choices.

PRIVATE DEVOTIONS

To know the way up and down the mountain, ask the one who made the mountain.

Prayer is an invisible tool that can make a very visible difference. Pray about everything, small or great. Stay in a prayerful attitude all the time. Develop the habit of listening, not just talking. Try forgetting any pre-established agenda you have, and consider praying this way: "God, show me clearly what are the wise choices and actions for me to take to assure other people's interests are best served."

And, be sure when you pray, to always, always thank God first for life's blessings. Take time to thank Him for blessings like health and family and answers to specific prayers.

I like to start and end my day in time alone with God, studying Wisdom's (the Bible's) pages, worshiping and praying. It's amazing how much better my attitude is when I do.

GROUP DEVOTIONS

Have daily devotions, prayer, Bible reading, and meditation in your home. Consider doing the same in your business by promoting voluntary devotion groups for employees. For home or business devotion settings, consider this format:

- Have one person read.

- Then, have a group prayer, with one person responsible for prayer.

- Ask members of the group for their spoken requests. Those who do not want to make their requests public can simply indicate their request is to remain unspoken (unspoken to the group, known to God, and prayed for by the group leader as an "unspoken request").

- Pray together, as a family or in your business.

- Pray for each other.

Peace of mind is found in praying and releasing people, relationships, things, and decisions to God, not in worrying and fretting over them.

KNEELING

If our dreams are honorable and spiritually born, we dream wisely and insure our success, as we allow God's partnership along our path of life. Dreams that are honorable and spiritually born, are birthed on bended knee.

WHEN I HAD NO PLACE TO GO, I WENT TO MY KNEES.
—*Abraham Lincoln*

INTERCESSION: LOVE ON IT'S KNEES IN PRAYER.
—*Unknown*

WHEN LIFE KNOCKS YOU TO YOUR KNEES, AND IT WILL, WHY, GET UP! IF IT KNOCKS YOU TO YOUR KNEES AGAIN, AS IT WILL, WELL, ISN'T THAT THE BEST POSITION FROM WHICH TO PRAY?
—*Ethel Barrymore*

A MAN NEVER STANDS TALLER THAN WHEN HE IS ON HIS KNEES.
—*Unknown*

CERTAIN THOUGHTS ARE PRAYERS. THERE ARE MOMENTS WHEN, WHATEVER BE THE ATTITUDE OF THE BODY, THE SOUL IS ON ITS KNEES.
—*Victor Hugo*

IF YOUR KNEES ARE KNOCKING, KNEEL ON THEM.
—*Unknown*

ASKING

Prayer is effective only when it is an activity, rather than an ideal.

Prayer is one of the few things that really matter.

When you pray, dream a while, release your worries, face your fears, bare your soul and open wide your spirit to hope and a brighter future.

PRAYER IS NOT A SUBSTITUTE FOR WORK, THINKING, WATCHING, SUFFERING, OR GIVING; PRAYER IS A SUPPORT FOR ALL OTHER EFFORTS.
—George Buttrick

THEY TELL ABOUT A FIFTEEN-YEAR-OLD BOY IN AN ORPHANS' HOME WHO HAD AN INCURABLE STUTTER. ONE SUNDAY THE MINISTER WAS DETAINED AND THE BOY VOLUNTEERED TO SAY THE PRAYER IN HIS STEAD. HE DID IT PERFECTLY, TOO, WITHOUT A SINGLE STUTTER. LATER HE EXPLAINED, "I DON'T STUTTER WHEN I TALK TO GOD. HE LOVES ME."
—Bennett Cerf

ASK, AND IT SHALL BE GIVEN YOU; SEEK, AND YE SHALL FIND; KNOCK, AND IT SHALL BE OPENED UNTO YOU.
—Jesus

GOD HEARS THE PRAYER OF A RIGHTEOUS PERSON. THE DIVINE DELIGHTS IN THEIR PRAYERS AND THOSE OF THE AFFLICTED AND THE DESTITUTE.
—King David

ANYONE WHO IMAGINES HE CAN SIMPLY BEGIN MEDITATING WITHOUT PRAYING FOR THE DESIRE AND THE GRACE TO DO SO, WILL SOON GIVE UP.
—Thomas Merton

DO NOT MAKE PRAYER A MONOLOGUE - MAKE IT A CONVERSATION.
—Unknown

Prayer leads to lives, dreams, relationships and families being saved, restored and reshaped.

ANYTHING LARGE ENOUGH FOR A WISH TO LIGHT UPON, IS LARGE ENOUGH TO HANG A PRAYER UPON.
-*George MacDonald*

To eliminate prejudice and bias, pray about them and then, make a conscious choice to neglect them with God's help.

CALLED OR NOT CALLED, GOD IS PRESENT.
— *carved on a stone tablet over Carl Jung's door*

PRAYERS OF GOD'S CHILDREN ARE THE INCENSE IN THE GOLDEN VIALS OF HEAVEN'S THRONE ROOM.
— *St. John*

A GRANDFATHER WAS WALKING THROUGH HIS YARD WHEN HE HEARD HIS GRANDDAUGHTER REPEATING THE ALPHABET IN A TONE OF VOICE THAT SOUNDED LIKE A PRAYER. HE ASKED HER WHAT SHE WAS DOING. THE LITTLE GIRL EXPLAINED: "I'M PRAYING, BUT I CAN'T THINK OF EXACTLY THE RIGHT WORDS, SO I'M JUST SAYING ALL THE LETTERS, AND GOD WILL PUT THEM TOGETHER FOR ME, BECAUSE HE KNOWS WHAT I'M THINKING.
— *Charles B. Vaughan*

SEEKING

Choice is a powerful gift from God. Use your choice prayerfully, respectfully, wisely, hopefully, and honorably.

Draw close to God and He will draw close to you. Prayer is as close as it gets, in this life!

A single moment in God's presence is worth a thousand anywhere else!

The wise always seek their Creator's guidance.

A wholesome life is the best model. Prayer is at the center of a wholesome life.

Highest spirituality is who we are as a result of a direct connection to God and absolute faith and trust in the One True God. It is not about doctrine, rules or what we can become or do, absent that connection.

Knowing God results in every other kind of understanding.

> I HAVE NOT THE COURAGE TO SEARCH THROUGH BOOKS FOR BEAUTIFUL PRAYERS... UNABLE EITHER TO SAY THEM ALL OR CHOOSE BETWEEN THEM, I DO AS A CHILD WOULD DO WHO CANNOT READ—I SAY JUST WHAT I WANT TO SAY TO GOD, QUITE SIMPLY, AND HE NEVER FAILS TO UNDERSTAND.
> —*St. Therese of Lisieux*

> GOD WARMS HIS HANDS AT MAN'S HEART WHEN HE PRAYS.
> —*Unknown*

> PRAYER IS THE WING WHEREWITH THE SOUL FLIES TO HEAVEN, AND MEDITATION THE EYE WHEREWITH WE SEE GOD.
> —*Ambrose of Milan*

> SEEK NOT TO UNDERSTAND THAT YOU MAY BELIEVE, BUT BELIEVE THAT YOU MAY UNDERSTAND.
> —*St. Augustine*

KNOCKING

Search for God's higher thoughts, through prayer, study of Scripture and meditation.

Endurance in prayer pays big dividends—now and in eternity.

Prayer is a very effective way to create a kinder world.

PRAYER IS NOT CONQUERING GOD'S RELUCTANCE, BUT TAKING HOLD OF GOD'S WILLINGNESS.
—*Phillips Brooks*

PRAYER IS NEVER AN ACCEPTABLE SUBSTITUTE FOR OBEDIENCE. THE SOVEREIGN LORD ACCEPTS NO OFFERING FROM HIS CREATURES THAT IS NOT ACCOMPANIED BY OBEDIENCE.
—*A. W. Tozer*

PRAYER COVERS THE WHOLE OF MAN'S LIFE. THERE IS NO THOUGHT, FEELING, YEARNING, OR DESIRE, HOWEVER LOW, TRIFLING, OR VULGAR WE MAY DEEM IT, WHICH IF IT AFFECTS OUR REAL INTEREST OR HAPPINESS, WE MAY NOT LAY BEFORE GOD AND BE SURE OF SYMPA-THY. HIS NATURE IS SUCH THAT OUR OFTEN COMING DOES NOT TIRE HIM. THE WHOLE BURDEN OF THE WHOLE LIFE OF MAN MAY BE ROLLED ON TO GOD AND NOT WEARY HIM, THOUGH IT HAS WEARIED MAN.
—*Henry Ward Beecher*

EVERYTHING IS POSSIBLE FOR THE PERSON WHO BELIEVES AND PUTS THEIR WHOLE TRUST IN GOD.
—*Jesus*

History records over and over, a nation is more powerful when it unites in sincere prayer to God than when it marshals and channels its resources into weapons of defense and warfare.

[WE SEEK] A CONSTITUTIONAL AMENDMENT TO PERMIT VOLUNTARY SCHOOL PRAYER. GOD SHOULD NEVER HAVE BEEN EXPELLED FROM AMERICA'S CLASSROOMS IN THE FIRST PLACE.
—*Ronald Wilson Reagan*

Simple prayers move The Divine to move and remove mountains in our lives.

WE HAVE REALLY LEARNED HOW TO PRAY WHEN WE REALIZE THAT PRAYER IS A PRIVILEGE RATHER THAN A DUTY.
—*Unknown*

HE WHO HAS CEASED TO PRAY HAS LOST A GREAT FRIEND.
—*Richard L. Evans*

PLANTING

It is wise to plant seeds in prayer today.

ALL THE FLOWERS OF
ALL THE TOMORROWS
ARE IN THE SEEDS OF
TODAY.
—*Chinese Proverb*

BY BELIEVING IN ROSES,
ONE BRINGS THEM TO
BLOOM.
—*French Proverb*

PERSONAL PRAYER, IT SEEMS TO ME, IS ONE OF THE SIMPLEST NECESSITIES OF LIFE, AS BASIC TO THE INDIVIDUAL AS SUNSHINE, FOOD AND WATER—AND AT TIMES, OF COURSE, MORE SO. BY PRAYER I MEAN AN EFFORT TO GET IN TOUCH WITH THE INFINITE. WE KNOW THAT OUR PRAYERS ARE IMPERFECT. OF COURSE THEY ARE. WE ARE IMPERFECT HUMAN BEINGS. A THOUSAND EXPERIENCES HAVE CONVINCED ME BEYOND ROOM OF DOUBT THAT PRAYER MULTIPLIES THE STRENGTH OF THE INDIVIDUAL AND BRINGS WITHIN THE SCOPE OF HIS CAPABILITIES ALMOST ANY CONCEIVABLE OBJECTIVE.
—*Dwight D. Eisenhower*

Prayer may be properly viewed as spiritual mealtime. In fact, prayer is fuel for the soul, a spiritual lifeline analogous to blood as our physical lifeline. Just as the body cannot survive without new blood, the spirit must have the fresh fuel of prayer several times a day.

Nourishment and strength from God through prayer and meditation on Eternal Truth, are soul food that assures fruitful spiritual growth.

Pray for heaven's dew to fall on the earth and your dry and thirsty ground.

The life of significance is the one that thirsts after God. Its' passion is to know Him intimately.

FOR THOSE WHO HAVE HIDDEN FELLOWSHIP WITH GOD, LIFE IS A CONTINUOUS FEAST.
—*S.G. Degraff*

LET US NOT GO FASTER THAN GOD. IT IS OUR EMPTINESS AND OUR THIRST THAT HE NEEDS, NOT OUR PLENITUDE.
—*Jacques Maritain*

WISE DIRECTION

Wisdom enables us—with guidance and tools for decision-making. Wisdom ennobles us—with compassion, thoughtfulness and generosity.

Applied to daily living and working, Wisdom has profound positive effects in the heart of our inner spiritual lives and outwardly, in our role and relationship conduct.

Guided by Wisdom, we discover life's greatest hopes and attain highest prosperity.

With Wisdom, we have the power to gain right result through purposeful planning.

Prayer is a good place to find Wisdom and gain powerful insight on how to best apply it in our daily living and working.

> PRAYING DOESN'T CHANGE GOD, IT CHANGES ME.
> —C.S. Lewis

FATHER, WE THANK YOU, ESPECIALLY FOR LETTING ME FLY THIS FLIGHT ... FOR THE PRIVILEGE OF BEING ABLE TO BE IN THIS POSITION, TO BE IN THIS WONDROUS PLACE, SEEING ALL THESE MANY STARTLING, WONDERFUL THINGS THAT YOU HAVE CREATED.
—L. Gordon Cooper, Jr., US astronaut

In prayer, Scripture reading and meditation, God shines the light on the path where we should go, gives us courage, guides our steps as we travel and imparts clear vision and sure hope.

The value of prayer is proven in many ways. For instance, Divine insight received in prayer is a beam of illumination directed into an otherwise dark or confused corner of the human mind and heart.

Life can be a beautiful journey when we pray about everything big or small and open our hearts to Truth and the influence of God.

Where we choose to place our attention has a great influence on the direction of our life. Thus, prayer can only influence our life path, when it is a matter of priority in our daily living.

We can choose to change the direction of our lives and when we do, it's a wise idea to ask God for the roadmap.

To know the way up and down the mountain, ask the One who made the mountain.

As we grow and mature, we learn that ends, good-byes, and loss are as much a part of life and love as beginnings, greetings, and gains. All of these inevitabilities create meaningful turning points in our lives. With Divine guidance, we choose to perceive them as opportunities for change and growth.

With spiritual roots and wings, our children have a strong sense of who they are and the power to take them to the places they were created to go. Teaching them the power of prayer and importance to their future of a devout prayer life, is at the core of wise child rearing.

Inspired and guided by God, we are eagles, able to fly above clouds and life's storms and soar to make our highest dreams and hopes reality.

TOOLS

Prayer is an invisible tool
that can make a very visible difference.

Prayer is a vital life tool because
it is a vital point of connection to God.

Connected to God's love and power through prayer,
Divine love and power become tools evident in our
roles and relationships, impacting each in wonderful
and awesome ways.

Our highest purpose is goodness achieved as we are
used as tools in Divine hands. Prayer time gives us the
opportunity to surrender and God the opportunity to
pour His goodness into us.

Prayer is the key to the door of intimacy with God.

A person, relationship, family and business that soars and lands safely is equipped
with wings of prayer and built of love.

Parents model adult behavior to children. This is the primary way children learn to
be adults. Model wise actions for your children to help them find a hopeful future.
A devout prayer life is one of the wisest, most hopeful models for parenting.

> PRAYER IS MORE THAN MEDITATION. IN MEDITATION THE SOURCE OF STRENGTH IS ONE'S SELF. WHEN ONE PRAYS HE GOES TO A SOURCE OF STRENGTH GREATER THAN HIS OWN.
> —*Madame Chiang Kai-Shek*

> PRAYER IS NOT AN OLD WOMAN'S IDLE AMUSEMENT. PROPERLY UNDERSTOOD AND APPLIED, IT IS THE MOST POTENT INSTRUMENT OF ACTION. PRAYER IS THE KEY OF THE MORNING AND THE BOLT OF THE EVENING.
> —*Mahatma Gandhi*

Prayer and study of and meditation on Eternal Truth are the points of connection to The One who created highest Wisdom, through which we obtain the tools to master daily living.

SERVICE

Our life is a special gift from above. What we do with it is our gift back. Prayer is among the best gifts we can give others.

Prayer helps us strike a proper balance between Heaven's daily calling to introspection and contemplation and Earth's practical life.

Unqualified uniqueness and limitless potential live in every child. Prayer is one of the vital spiritual formation tools of parenting and mentoring, for nurturing uniqueness and assuring potential is realized. Children need to learn to pray. The best model is praying with them.

Personal example is the best opportunity to influence others. The proof of how influential others regard us, can be seen in whether or not they ask us to pray for them and their needs.

Live to serve others. The freedoms to love and serve each other cannot be taken from us. Praying for others and their needs is a wonderful way to exercise that freedom.

Significance is found in serving others. One of the easiest and yet most effective ways to serve others is to love them enough to pray for them daily.

PEOPLE

People care how much we care, far more than how much we know. Praying for others and their needs proves we care.

Prayer is a vital means of bringing God into our and others' lives and for bringing ourselves and others to God.

We need to make the godly our heroes, those who are truly good, stand for right, and behind the scenes are prayer warriors of great faith who spend a great deal of their life on bent knees, rather than strutting their stuff and serving themselves.

Helping a child reach their potential requires time, effort and involves emotional trials. But, serving as guides and mirrors—being prayer warriors and reflecting in our examples God's hope, love and special plans for each of these special hearts—is a reward no other endeavor offers!

Those who pray together, stay together. Prayer is the bond that holds together lives, relationships, families and organizations.

Prayer has ripple effects in the lake of lives. Some waves are slow, gentle, and easy. Others are not so. Both are good for all whose lives the waves of our prayers touch.

Honor others by asking for their prayers and help when you need them.

Let God, others and their needs be the center of your prayers.

PRAYER IS LESS ABOUT CHANGING THE WORLD THAN IT IS ABOUT CHANGING OURSELVES.
—David J. Wolpe

LIVE AMONG MEN AS THOUGH GOD WERE WATCHING. TALK TO GOD AS THOUGH MEN WERE LISTENING.
—Unknown

HOLDING THE HEART OF ANOTHER IN THE COMFORTING HANDS OF PRAYER IS A PRICELESS ACT OF LOVE.
—Janet L. Weaver

SUCCESS

The exceptional life is the one connected at the heart to God. Those individuals see through God's eyes, love with His heart and make decisions based on His higher thinking.

Internal wisdom produces eternal success.

The path of highest success is lit with reflections. Reflections of Divine truth and love, shining brightly and warmly to light our way. Reflections of those who have traveled before us who share their memories, cautions and words of wisdom. Reflections of every traveling heart, young or old–contemplating, questioning, evaluating and praying along this wondrous journey.

Destiny is the consequence of choice, not chance. Choosing to pray can change destinies.

Life's greatest accomplishments are the result of reckless abandon to God working through us.

Those who most powerfully influence are prayer warriors who live simple, godly lives.

True greatness is leaving the impression of God on all we influence. Those who have devout prayer lives focused on others have the most influence, in heaven and on earth.

Highest prosperity results from becoming exceptional at the ordinary, but vital things of life, like prayer.

The mighty tree yielding the fruit of success began a seedling of hope, from a quiet moment of sincere prayer.

> HE HAS ACHIEVED SUCCESS WHO HAS LIVED WELL, LAUGHED OFTEN AND LOVED MUCH.
> —Mrs. A. J. Stanley

When we take the steps to restore our connection to God, The Divine Spirit literally comes to live in us, creating a brand new person inside and beginning a new life. Divine goodness, attitudes, skill and power then reside in us. Effectively, we are clothed with a new inner nature of greatness that outwardly produces true success in our lives and all we influence.

Hopeful desires, thoughts and attitudes that lead to success, begin in prayer and meditation.

Confidence comes from the inside–from your heart. Prayer builds inner confidence. Depend on prayer and what is inside you to achieve true success, not what is outside.

Quiet determination gained through constant connection to God, is the inner rope that can keep us hanging on, taking us to the top of the mountains of success others quit climbing long ago.

An intimate relationship with God will move your life upward to highest significance.

Leaders who achieve lasting success follow these essential principles of Eternal Truth:

> *Have disaffection for what is, passion for what can be*
>
> *Seek God first to understand, rather than to be understood*
>
> *Power and position create opportunity for service*
>
> *Elevate people and relationships above anything else*
>
> *Serve graciously and humbly*
>
> *Ask nicely, show appreciation, and correct pleasantly*
>
> *Give until it hurts, go the extra mile and forgive*
>
> *Before deciding, ask God, "Is this best for all concerned?"*

LISTENING

Close your eyes, listen to your heart... and remember.
Speak–pray–to–the Divine who has created you.
Reconnect and become anew.

Into the silence of our hearts, the Divine speaks.
Don't be afraid of silence.

Silence is the doorway to a peaceful state, the opportunity to block out the noise of modern life and the critical window of time in prayer, for listening to what God is saying to and through us.

Being alone regularly can be a wonderful gift. It's a great opportunity to learn more about ourselves and also, to listen to God.

Listening is the first step in learning. That is especially true in prayer.

Yes, no or wait are all Divine answers to our prayers.

Often, God's best answer is no. Too frequently we demand and get less than God's best.

> IN PRAYER IT IS BETTER TO HAVE A HEART WITHOUT WORDS THAN WORDS WITHOUT A HEART.
> —*John Bunyan*

> GOD IS THE FRIEND OF SILENCE. TREES, FLOWERS, GRASS GROW IN SILENCE. SEE THE STARS, MOON, AND SUN, HOW THEY MOVE IN SILENCE.
> —*Mother Teresa*

Believe in God, even in times of what seems total silence. That's a good time to listen.

Prayer is where we get our marching orders. Listen carefully, before marching.

God is never too busy to hear and answer our prayers.

PRAYER IS TALKING WITH GOD AND TELLING HIM YOU LOVE HIM, CONVERSING WITH GOD ABOUT ALL THE THINGS THAT ARE IMPORTANT IN LIFE, BOTH LARGE AND SMALL, AND BEING ASSURED THAT HE IS LISTENING.
—*C. Neil Strait*

A heart and ears turned upward mark the beginning of hearing God and finding the path of life He wants us to follow. Otherwise, we are destined to remain indifferent to that which matters most.

By tuning out the chatter of the head, praying and then, meditating on the insightful messages of our childlike heart, we make wise choices that stand the test of time.

Listening to God we are assured of living unafraid, in peace and safety.

PEACE

With Divine guidance and the gifts of Wisdom, Honor and Hope, we find peace and simplicity that allow us to handle our complex lives with assured faith and strong character.

No matter where we find ourselves, we can always find rest, peace and discover new strengths–safely embraced in the sanctuary of Divine love.

LORD, MAKE ME AN INSTRUMENT OF YOUR PEACE. WHERE THERE IS HATRED LET ME SOW LOVE; WHERE THERE IS INJURY, PARDON; WHERE THERE IS DOUBT, FAITH; WHERE THERE IS DESPAIR, HOPE; WHERE THERE IS DARKNESS, LIGHT; AND WHERE THERE IS SADNESS, JOY. O DIVINE MASTER, GRANT THAT I MAY NOT SO MUCH SEEK TO BE CONSOLED AS TO CONSOLE; TO BE UNDERSTOOD AS TO UNDERSTAND; TO BE LOVED AS TO LOVE. FOR IT IS IN THE GIVING THAT WE RECEIVE; IT IS IN THE PARDONING THAT WE ARE PARDONED; AND IT IS IN THE DYING THAT WE ARE BORN TO ETERNAL LIFE.
—*St. Francis of Assisi*

THE FOUNTAIN OF TRANQUILITY IS WITHIN OURSELVES; LET US KEEP IT PURE.
—*Phocian*

KEEP US, LORD, SO AWAKE IN THE DUTIES OF OUR CALLINGS THAT WE MAY SLEEP IN THY PEACE AND WAKE IN THY GLORY.
—*John Donne*

Peace found in prayer overcomes our doubt and fear.

In the midst of life's storms, God's voice brings us peace and strength.

THE PEACE OF GOD WILL KEEP YOUR HEART AND MIND.
—*St. Paul*

LOVE

Love is the centerpiece of prayer.

A legacy of love and prayer is more valuable and far more enduring than one of money and things.

MOST MEN PRAY FOR POWER, THE STRENGTH TO DO THINGS. FEW PEOPLE PRAY FOR LOVE, THE QUALITY TO BE SOMEONE.
—*Robert D. Foster*

FORGIVENESS

Prayer is a good time, for saying "God, I'm sorry," and for examining our hearts to determine who we need to forgive and who we need to ask for forgiveness.

By seeking guidance and allowing God to work through us, we can initiate limitless forgiveness.

Look inside, do an honest accounting and write down the unwise things that have caused you to fall short of your best. Ask God to forgive you, forgive yourself and others and sincerely ask others for forgiveness. Then, at dawn, leave the past behind, get into the future changing what can be changed, living Eternal Truth, nothing but that Truth, so help you God.

The true test of character is not a tally of a person's mistakes. Rather, it is the manner in which mistakes are handled–admitting the error, recognizing how it was made, and committing to change. In prayer, we can obtain the wisdom, courage and strength to do all three.

> AND FORGIVE US OUR TRESPASSES AS WE FORGIVE THOSE WHO TRESPASS AGAINST US...
> —*The Lord's Prayer*

FAITH

Prayer and faith are keys to a better life.

The solidity of our faith and how we choose to care, act and handle decisions determines our balance, in an "always in motion modern society".

Faith works through prayer and love.

When we pray, Jesus taught it is essential we believe.

Belief is a key to healing, recovery, renewal, and future achievement.

FAITH IS A GIFT OF GOD AND GROWS THROUGH PRAYER, AS DO HOPE AND LOVE—AND THOSE THREE ARE THE MAIN VIRTUES OF THE INTERIOR LIFE.
—*Mother Teresa*

IF SOMEONE IS SICK, PUT A DROP OF OIL ON THEIR FOREHEAD (AS A SYMBOL OF GOD'S SPIRIT AND HEALING POWER) AND CALL ON THE LORD TO HEAL THEM. AND, THIS PRAYER, IF OFFERED IN FAITH, WILL HEAL THE PERSON, FOR GOD WILL MAKE THEM WELL.
—*St. James*

FAITH IS AN ACTIVITY; IT IS SOMETHING THAT HAS TO BE APPLIED.
—*Corrie Ten Boon*

FAITH IS A HIGHER FACULTY THAN REASON.
—*Henry Bailey*

ETERNAL TRUTH

Eternal Truth always points upward, reminding us of our higher purpose.

Eternal Truth opens your eyes to new Beauty and your ears to new Music.

Eternal Truth releases you to a heightened reality of meaning and Hope.

Eternal Truth is found and learned in vital connections with The Divine, especially in solitary times of prayer, Scripture reading and quiet meditation and reflection.

Recognize and be filled with Eternal Truth when you hear it. This will bring you wisdom.

Believe on Eternal Truth through faith. This will bring you hope.

Act on Eternal Truth. This will bring you peace and joy.

Take care to assure your requests of God are consistent with Eternal Truth.

Two of the best lessons embedded within the storms of life, are the need for constant attention to prayer and making our choices based on Eternal Truth.

The most important step we can ever take to shape our destiny, responsibly and confidently, is first making a serious commitment to the principles and values of Eternal Truth.

Prayer is both a central principle and important value of Eternal Truth.

God's laws are eternal truths that protect us, make us wise and give us joy and light. They warn us away from harm and give lasting success to those who apply them. In prayer and meditation time, God teaches us those truths, writing them on our hearts so that in daily living and working they are our respected guides.

Eternal truths are joyous treasures and the wisdom and understanding to honorably apply them, is more valuable than silver or gold. Such know-how is often an answer to earnest prayer.

A life of true honor is one lived by the standards of Eternal Truth that become part of our inner person, through careful study, quiet meditation and prayerfully seeking Divine guidance.

JOY

Prayer opens our hearts to the beauty and possibilities around us. And, it is there in prayer we can rediscover and reclaim laughter, joy, peace and immense hope of a brighter, better future.

The highest joys and most exquisite pleasures of life are found only in God's presence.

Those who truly seek God live in joy.

HOPE

Faith and hope are our heart's eyes and higher intellect, the spiritual vision and knowledge that drive fear from our spirit as we soar beyond doubt. Prayer is a vital pipeline that delivers Divine faith and hope to our soul.

> HOPE IS A THING WITH FEATHERS / THAT PERCHES ON THE SOUL, / AND SINGS THE TUNE WITHOUT WORDS, / AND NEVER STOPS AT ALL.
> —Emily Dickinson

Bathed in tears of sorrow and prayer, the past becomes a beautiful memory our heart holds forever and the touchstone to a brighter, better future full of hope and many possibilities.

The most hopeful lives are those lived by faith in and prayer to God.

> PRAYER IS A WINE WHICH MAKES GLAD THE HEART OF MAN.
> —St. Bernard

To find constant hope and happiness, look up.

The eternal glow of the Divine Light provides wisdom, truth and hope to all who seek this brightly-lit path of true success. Prayer is the best way to find it.

Looking up reveals a brighter, better future. Keeping our gaze upward, fixed and steady, we can be sure with God's great help we can do anything.

Facing the storms of life and their pain, in prayer, Scripture reading and meditation, we can understand them better and learn the lessons embedded in them. Then we can see the dawning of a new day, one where we have the opportunity to take wise and honorable action toward a bright, hopeful future.

> THE VALUE OF PERSISTENT PRAYER IS NOT THAT HE WILL HEAR US . . . BUT THAT WE WILL FINALLY HEAR HIM.
> —*William McGill*

Storms of life are opportunities to pause...

- reconnect to God, ourselves and others

- learn and grow from them

- and discover within them strengths and future blessings.

God is a tested and true help in troubled times.

God makes a way, even when it seems there is no way!

THANKFULNESS

Expressing gratitude for all we have and experience is a powerful spiritual exercise.

Choose gratitude, and you will attract abundance into your life.

Pray with lofty praise of the Divine and genuine thanksgiving to Him, for life's blessings.

Praise God for providing every good gift that has and will come your way.

Exalt the Divine for his mercy.

Each day, thank God and pray for your spouse, children, parents, relatives, friends, neighbors, employer and on the job associates.

Praying over our meals before eating, asking God to bless us and the food, is a wonderful way to express our thanks and gratitude to God for His blessings. It is also a wise way to protect the body from sickness and disease-bearing agents in the food.

> ONE SINGLE GRATEFUL THOUGHT RAISED TO HEAVEN IS THE MOST PERFECT PRAYER.
> —*G. E. Lessing*

> THOSE WHO THANK GOD MUCH ARE TRULY WEALTHY. SO OUR INNER HAPPINESS DEPENDS NOT ON WHAT WE EXPERIENCE BUT ON THE DEGREE OF OUR GRATITUDE TO GOD, WHATEVER THE EXPERIENCE.
> —*Albert Schweitzer*

God's loving-kindness is wonderful and His mercy is plentiful and very tender. Remember in prayer to praise and thank God for these and all the blessings that come from Him.

LET US THANK GOD HEARTILY AS OFTEN AS WE PRAY THAT WE HAVE HIS SPIRIT IN US TO TEACH US TO PRAY. THANKSGIVING WILL DRAW OUR HEARTS OUT TO GOD AND KEEP US ENGAGED WITH HIM; IT WILL TAKE OUR ATTENTION FROM OURSELVES AND GIVE THE SPIRIT ROOM IN OUR HEARTS.
— *Andrew Murray*

OUR THANKS TO GOD SHOULD ALWAYS PRECEDE OUR REQUESTS.
— *Unknown*

LIFT UP YOUR HEARTS TO HIM, SOMETIMES EVEN AT YOUR MEALS, AND WHEN YOU ARE IN COMPANY; THE LEAST LITTLE REMEMBRANCE WILL ALWAYS BE ACCEPTABLE TO HIM. YOU NEED NOT CRY VERY LOUD; HE IS NEARER TO US THAN WE ARE AWARE.
— *Brother Lawrence*

MODEL

Consider this model prayer, a paraphrase of Jesus' simple, but powerfully profound teaching on prayer.

Heavenly Father, you are holy and holy is your name. Lord, I thank you and praise you today for your power, wisdom, kindness, justice, mercy and truth.

Thank You for the manifold blessings freely and abundantly given me. I acknowledge you as the source of those.

I commit myself and choose again today to put our relationship first. Come and be the ruler of my life, make your throne the center of my soul. Rekindle in me today a childlike trust in and a reverence for You, that are seen in doing everything I can to please You. Help me to be as obedient as the angels.

Help me today to bring honor and glory to You, making a difference in other peoples' lives. Let every person on and off the job see You quietly at work in me. May that bring them faith and hope and increase their desire to be in partnership with You. Bring every person I impact into harmonious relationship with You.

Forgive me, according to how I forgive. Give me the grace to forgive and forget, the courage and good sense to seek forgiveness for every offense I have yet to ask pardon for and the willingness to make amends.

I trust You today, for today's needs.

Protect my loved ones and me, from the influence of evil. Turn darkness into light, as Your light shines within and through me. Help me to apply your Eternal Truth today to avoid traps, snares and pitfalls and to be safe, secure and attain highest prosperity.

You alone are worthy of my praise and worship and I freely give them to You.

Amen.